J
616.9
MON
Monroe, Judy
Influenza and other viruses.

Influenza and Other Viruses

By Judy Monroe

Consultant:
Charles Grose, MD
Professor of Pediatrics
University of Iowa Hospital

Perspectives on Disease and Illness

LifeMatters
an imprint of Capstone Press
Mankato, Minnesota

LifeMatters books are published by Capstone Press
PO Box 669 • 151 Good Counsel Drive • Mankato, Minnesota 56002
http://www.capstone-press.com

Printed in the United States of America

Library of Congress Cataloging-in-Publication Data
Monroe, Judy.
     Influenza and other viruses / by Judy Monroe.
                    p.   cm. — (Perspectives on disease and illness)
     Includes bibliographical references and index.
     ISBN 0-7368-1025-0
     1. Virus diseases—Juvenile literature. 2. Influenza—Juvenile literature. 3. Cold (Disease)—Juvenile literature. [1. Viruses. 2. Virus diseases. 3. Influenza. 4. Cold (Disease). 5. Diseases.] I. Title. II. Series.
     RC114.5 .M66 2002
     616.9′25—dc21

                                                            00-013233
                                                            CIP

Summary: Explains what viruses are, how they cause disease, and how they are spread. Discusses how the body works to fight viral illnesses and gives suggestions for treatment and prevention. Includes information on the direction of research for new drugs and vaccines.

Staff Credits
Rebecca Aldridge, editor; Adam Lazar, designer; Kim Danger, photo researcher

Photo Credits
Cover: ©DigitalVision, left; ©Artville/Clair Alaska, middle; ©Capstone Press/Gary Sundermeyer, right; The Stock Market/©Howard Sochurek, bottom
©DigitalVision, 21
International Stock/©Michael Agliolo, 12; ©Giovanni Lunardi, 17; ©Mike Agliolo, 56; ©Peter Tenzer, 59
Photo Network/42, ©Patti McConville, 22; ©Mary Messenger, 45
©Stockbyte, 35, 37
Uniphoto/Pictor/©Mark Reinstein, 7
Visuals Unlimited/©Science VU, 8, 30, 32; ©Veronina Burmeister, 14; ©Robert Calentine, 25; ©Kim Fennema, 48; ©Jeff Greenberg, 51

Table of Contents

Chapter Overview

Viruses are simple, tiny things, but they're one of the body's worst enemies. They can cause many serious illnesses.

Ancient people had various beliefs about what caused diseases.

Viruses were unknown until the 1890s. Researchers first saw viruses through the electron microscope in the 1940s.

Chapter 1

What Are Viruses?

"Achoo!" Teshia blew her nose and stuffed the tissue into her jacket pocket. "I wish my nose would stop running. And my throat hurts a little," she said to her friend Rosa.

Teshia, Age 15

"I hope you don't get the flu like you did last year. Remember how sick you were?" Rosa held open a large, black bag while Teshia raked leaves into it.

Teshia coughed. "You're right. It happened right before winter break. The worst part was missing your big sledding party. I sure don't want the flu again!"

At a Glance

Just how tiny are viruses? One particular virus measures only two-millionths of an inch across.

Fall is the time of year when millions of people like Teshia are sneezing, coughing, and blowing their nose. It's the beginning of the flu and cold season. Viruses cause both flu and colds.

What Viruses Are

Viruses are simple, tiny things that can cause disease. They're so small that thousands can fit on the tip of a pin. Viruses come in many shapes. Some look like a thin rod, while others are round and fluffy. Some viruses are shaped like a brick, a bullet, or a many-sided crystal. Viruses are everywhere: on the ground, in water, and in the air.

Viruses have an inner core of genetic material and are coated by a shell of protein. They cannot live on their own and depend on living cells to survive and reproduce. They invade healthy cells and take over, copying themselves and sometimes multiplying greatly. When virus-infected cells spread in the body, they can cause various illnesses. Diseases that viruses cause include flu, colds, measles, mumps, rabies, and AIDS.

Viruses are specific in the kind of cells they invade. Only certain viruses can invade certain cells. For example, a virus passed from the bite of an infected animal causes rabies. The rabies virus attacks only cells of the central nervous system.

Viruses can survive outside living cells but then cannot multiply or destroy cells. Viruses are considered dormant when they're outside of living cells.

Fall is the beginning of the flu and cold season. Both illnesses are caused by a virus.

Mystery of the Virus

Ancient people didn't know about viruses, so they came up with various reasons to explain why people became ill. Some people thought magic spells caused diseases. Others thought that if they did something wrong, they would get sick. Still others said that people became ill when they lost their soul from the body. Another theory was that the gods caused diseases.

Hippocrates, the father of modern medicine (460–377 B.C.), is considered the greatest doctor of ancient times. He helped advance a new idea—that gods don't cause diseases. Instead, he thought things such as drinking water, the weather, and climate caused diseases.

Another key step in discovering viruses occurred in Delft, Holland. There, a merchant named Antonie van Leeuwenhoek (1632–1723), taught himself to make microscopes. He looked at substances such as rainwater and his own feces, or solid body waste. He also looked at tartar, the yellow substance that forms on teeth. Van Leeuwenhoek was the first person to see and write about bacteria and other small living things. However, viruses were too small to be seen through van Leeuwenhoek's microscopes.

British doctor Edward Jenner (1749–1823) developed the world's first vaccine against smallpox. This viral disease was a major cause of death in the 18th century. Vaccines are preparations of a killed or weakened virus. Today, as in Jenner's time, they're injected, or shot, by needle into the body. The vaccine causes the body to build up antibodies that fight the virus. This protects the body against the virus without the person getting sick. If the person is exposed to that virus in the future, he or she does not get the disease. That's because antibodies remain in a person's body. Although Jenner's vaccine worked, no one knew why.

French chemist and biologist Louis Pasteur (1822–1895) developed vaccines for several diseases, including rabies. Pasteur also proved that germs cause diseases. Germs are so small they can only be seen through a microscope. Viruses and bacteria are two kinds of germs.

Viruses Discovered

In 1892, a Russian, Dmitri Ivanovski, tried to discover why tobacco plants got sick with mosaic disease. This disease kills tobacco leaves. Ivanovski passed sap from diseased tobacco plants through many filters. At this time, these filters trapped all known bacteria. Yet the filtered sap still produced mosaic disease in new plants. So, Ivanovski's tests proved that other tiny disease-causing germs exist.

Myth: Because they're so small, viruses are weak.

Fact: Many viruses are tough. Some can live at a temperature of 200 degrees Fahrenheit (93.3 degrees Celsius) below freezing. Others will not collapse under a force that is 100,000 times greater than gravity. Certain viruses can live hundreds of years outside the human body.

Six years later in Germany, Friedrich Loeffler and Paul Frosch reported similar results for foot-and-mouth disease. Many cattle died from this deadly disease. The two men proved that something very small that wasn't bacteria caused foot-and-mouth disease. They called this tiny thing a virus. They also proved that this virus reproduced itself within infected cattle.

For the next 30 years, many viruses that grow in animals, plants, insects, and bacteria were discovered. By the early 1930s, scientists had developed many new methods for virology, or the study of viruses. For example, scientists could now grow many animal viruses in the laboratory.

Researchers finally saw viruses by the 1940s, thanks to the invention of a special microscope. This was called the electron microscope. It magnified objects 40,000 to 100,000 times their normal size. Now, scientists could study the size and shape of viruses in detail. The following decade, researchers discovered how viruses work in the body.

Points to Consider

What diseases can you think of that are caused by a virus?

Why do you think ancient people came up with many theories about the cause of diseases?

Some people still blame factors other than viruses and bacteria for diseases. What are some myths you have heard?

Chapter Overview

The five types of germs that cause communicable diseases in people are viruses, bacteria, rickettsias, fungi, and protozoans. Viruses are responsible for some of the most serious and sometimes deadly diseases.

The body has many ways to keep out harmful germs. The first lines of defense include the skin, tears, saliva, and mucus. Stomach juices, certain body cells, and fevers kill harmful germs, too.

The second line of defense against infections is the immune system. Various cells, tissues, and organs fight specific germs.

Viruses replicate by injecting their genetic material into cells. The virus makes copies of itself by using materials within these cells. The new viruses spread to other cells and make even more copies of the virus.

Germs can enter the body and cause disease by direct or indirect contact. Germs also can get in the body by contact with animals and eating or drinking foods that contain germs.

Chapter 2

Germs Attack, the Body Reacts

Kyle sneezed, then sneezed again. "Hey! Cover your nose and mouth when you sneeze. I'll get your cold if you keep sneezing like that," said Blong. The two friends were studying at Blong's house.

Kyle and Blong, Age 16

"Stop being a wimp," said Kyle. "You won't catch my cold. You take vitamins with your orange juice every morning."

"That might help, but I could still get sick. And I can't afford that right now. I've got to ace this test and then pull a double shift on my job this weekend. I'm taking Sheryl to the homecoming dance, so I need to make extra money. Please get the box of tissues in the bathroom. Then you can sneeze all you want."

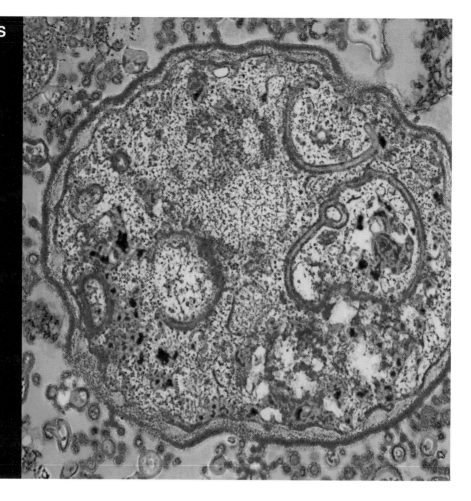

The AIDS virus is often deadly.

What Are Germs?

Each day, you're exposed to many germs. They are in the air, on surfaces, and in foods. Germs are so small that they can be seen only through a microscope. Some germs cause no problem for people and are helpful. Other germs can cause disease. Five types of germs cause communicable diseases. These are diseases that can be spread from person to person.

Viruses. These are the smallest and simplest germs. Many viruses cause diseases in people. Some of these diseases are serious, even deadly.

Bacteria. These tiny, one-celled, living organisms grow nearly everywhere. Bacteria can be helpful or harmful to people.

Rickettsias. These organisms multiply by invading the cells of living things. Most rickettsias are found in fleas, ticks, mites, and mice. Rickettsias cause diseases such as typhus and Rocky Mountain spotted fever. Symptoms of these diseases include headache, fever, and rashes. Rocky Mountain spotted fever can cause death if not treated early.

Fungi. Fungi are simple organisms that cannot make their own food. They live in people's hair, nails, and skin. Two diseases caused by fungi are athlete's foot and ringworm, both of which cause rashes.

Protozoans. These are single-celled organisms larger than bacteria. Most protozoans are harmless, but about 30 types cause disease in humans.

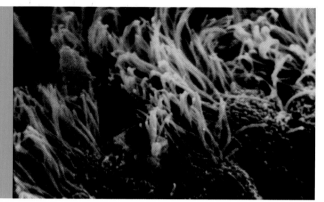

First Lines of Defense

The body has four types of first-line defenses against harmful germs. These defenses usually work well to keep germs from causing infection or disease.

Physical barriers. The main barrier to germs is the skin. Unbroken skin helps stop viruses from entering the body. However, germs can enter through a cut, scrape, or burn.

If viruses enter the body, the mucous membranes offer protection. Mucous membranes are a soft, slippery lining of many body parts. For example, they line the inside of the mouth, nose, and bronchial tubes that lead to the lungs. Mucous membranes create a sticky substance called mucus that traps and carries away germs. Some mucous membranes have cilia. These are tiny hairs that trap and sweep out germs.

Chemical barriers. Enzymes are proteins in tears and saliva that destroy germs. Tears also wash away germs from the eyes. Digestive juices in the stomach contain acids that destroy germs swallowed with foods or drinks.

After a virus invades the body, a race is on. First, the virus rapidly reproduces itself in body cells. Then, the body's immune system attacks the virus. The winner is determined within 10 to 14 days. If the immune system wins, the virus is killed. If the virus wins, the person becomes ill.

Body cells. If germs reach the bloodstream, certain white blood cells called phagocytes go to work. Phagocytes travel through the blood, group together, and then destroy germs.

Inflammatory response. Fever kills germs that cannot live when body temperature is higher than normal.

"I was reading in a teen magazine how I can help keep germs from getting into my body. **Cari, Age 14** One thing is to avoid too much sun. Ultraviolet rays from the sun can damage my skin, making it easier for germs to invade the body. Another thing I can do is to eat healthy foods. Lots of yellow and green vegetables and fruits can help keep my skin healthy."

Second Line of Defense: The Immune System

Most times, people remain healthy and do not get sick. Sometimes harmful germs get through a first line of defense. They enter the body and grow and multiply. Then, the immune system begins fighting to get rid of the harmful things that have entered the body.

Scientists have found two types of lymphocytes: B-cells and T-cells. Bone marrow, the soft tissue in the center of the bone, makes both cells. B-cells produce antibodies. T-cells attack germs and control the activity of B-cells and other parts of the immune system.

The immune system consists of a group of cells, tissues, and organs that fight specific germs. Lymphocytes are an important part of the immune system. Some of these white blood cells multiply and attack germs. Other lymphocytes make antibodies. These chemicals fight off harmful invaders. Each antibody fights one particular substance. If a germ enters the body, the immune system produces the correct antibodies to fight infection from that particular germ.

How Viruses Cause Disease

The immune system usually kills most viruses. Sometimes the immune system cannot handle a virus and the person becomes sick.

When a virus enters the body, it infects specific cells. For example, cold viruses infect cells in the nose and throat. These specific cells are called host cells. The virus injects its genetic material into the host cell. The virus makes copies of itself by using materials within the host cells. The new viruses spread to other cells and repeat the process.

How Diseases Are Spread

Germs enter the body and cause disease in four ways:

Direct contact. When someone touches an infected area, germs can be picked up. This includes touching infected skin and mucous membranes. It also includes sexual contact. For example, people can get HIV and herpes through sexual contact.

Sharing the same spoon is a form of indirect contact that can spread flu and cold viruses.

Indirect contact. When a person who is sick coughs or sneezes, infected drops of moisture are spread into the air. Someone close by could breathe in these germs. Sharing cups, utensils, and other personal items with a sick person also can spread germs. Some people cough into their hands and then handle a doorknob. Touching a doorknob after this happens is another example of indirect contact. Flu and cold viruses can be spread by indirect contact.

Contact with animals. The bite of an infected animal or insect can cause disease. Rabies is one virus spread this way.

Other contact. Germs enter the body if people drink liquids or eat foods that contain them. For this reason, food that isn't stored correctly or that is undercooked can be dangerous. Food poisoning can result.

Points to Consider

Before giving someone a shot, a doctor or nurse wipes the skin with alcohol. Why do you think this is done?

What are some ways you could avoid germs?

What do you think happens if a person's immune system stops working?

Chapter Overview

Both flu and colds are respiratory infections caused by viruses. Both are spread by direct and indirect contact. Colds usually affect only the upper respiratory system. Flu involves the entire body and can be more serious than colds.

Colds and flu share some general symptoms such as sore throat, runny nose, and a cough.

Flu symptoms usually are worse and last longer than cold symptoms. People with flu often have muscle and joint aches, a high temperature, and headache. Flu can be dangerous for children and seniors. It also can be dangerous for people with certain diseases and weakened immune systems. Sometimes flu can lead to other serious diseases, causing death.

Flu epidemics and pandemics have occurred in history and continue to strike. During flu outbreaks, many people get infected, and thousands have died.

Flu viruses mutate. This makes it hard to develop drugs to stop flu from spreading.

Chapter 3

Flu and Colds

Mia woke in the middle of the night. Her head pounded, and she coughed and coughed. **Mia, Age 14** Then she sneezed a few times. Her throat was so sore that she couldn't swallow. Even though it hurt to strain her voice, she called, "Mom!"

Seconds later, her mom flipped on the light. "Mom, I'm really sick. Can you give me some medicine?" Mia asked.

Mrs. Perez felt her daughter's forehead. "You feel a little warm." She left and came back with a thermometer, a glass of water, and a bottle of nonaspirin. First she took Mia's temperature. It was 100 degrees Fahrenheit, which meant Mia had a fever. Then she gave Mia a pill.

"You may have the flu or a cold. Let's see how you are in the morning," said Mrs. Perez as she tucked the covers up around Mia's neck.

Americans get about 1 billion colds each year.

Every year, about 10 to 20 percent of people in the United States are infected with the flu. About 16 percent of the people in Canada get the flu each year.

Alike, but Different

Does Mia have the flu or a cold? So far, Mia's symptoms match both illnesses. These symptoms include a sore throat, stuffy nose, and cough. Flu and colds are alike in other ways, too. Both illnesses are respiratory infections caused by viruses. Respiratory infections affect the body system that helps a person breathe. Both flu and colds are spread by direct and indirect contact.

Flu and colds differ in many ways. Scientists have counted more than 200 different cold viruses. They have found only three main types of flu viruses. These are types A, B, and C. Type A is the most common and severe. Type B is the second most common. Type C is the rarest. Because so many types of cold viruses exist, people are more likely to catch a cold than the flu.

Flu can be more serious than a cold. Colds usually affect only the upper respiratory system. Flu involves the entire body. Flu can be dangerous for young children and senior citizens or for people with lung or heart disease. It also can cause problems for people with certain diseases such as cancer or AIDS. These people may have a weakened immune system.

Flu is a major cause of illness and death in the United States. Each year, about 20,000 people die from the flu. In Canada, the flu was expected to kill about 4,500 people in the year 2001.

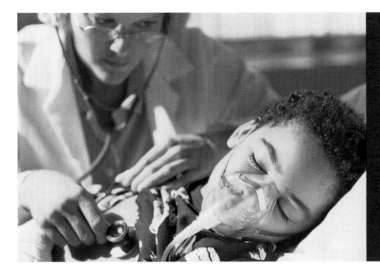

In the United States, more than 110,000 people are hospitalized with the flu each year.

Cold and Flu Symptoms

Most colds last less than one week. If Mia has a cold, she'll start to feel better within two to five days. People can catch colds any time of the year, but most colds occur in the fall and winter. Cold symptoms develop slowly. They usually appear in a day or two, not suddenly. Here are typical cold symptoms:

Stuffy or runny nose

Scratchy, sore throat

Hacking cough

Mild to moderate chest discomfort

No fever or low fever under 101 degrees Fahrenheit (F) or 38.3 degrees Celsius (C)

Slight tiredness

Headache

Itchy, irritated eyes

Loss of appetite

People who have the flu often have a variety of symptoms that may include extreme tiredness and headache.

People who have the flu usually feel sick for about a week and need another week to feel better again. Flu is common from late October through mid-April. The peak of flu season runs from late December through early March. Typical flu symptoms appear fast and can include:

Extreme tiredness (can last two to three weeks)

Chest discomfort

Cough

Stuffy or runny nose

Headache

Scratchy, sore throat

Fever higher than 101 degrees F (38.3 degrees C)

Achy and sick feeling all over the body

Chills

Irritated, watery eyes

Influenza comes from the Italian word *influenza*, which means "influence." People in the early 15th century blamed the illness on the "influence" of the stars, moon, and sun.

Did You
Know?

Flu and Cold Dangers

The flu can lead to other problems. Ear infections can develop, leading to ear pain and fever. Sometimes the air passages in the nose and face become infected. This is called sinusitis. Symptoms include headaches, pain around the nose, coughing, and other cold symptoms that last more than two weeks.

Flu can lead to other serious diseases such as pneumonia, which is inflammation of the lungs. This means the lungs are red, hot, and swollen. A person with pneumonia runs a high fever, breathes quickly, coughs, and feels extremely tired. This painful disease causes many deaths each year. Flu, combined with pneumonia, is the sixth leading cause of death in the United States every year.

Bronchitis is another illness that can develop from the flu. Bronchitis is an infection of the two large bronchial tubes that lead into the lungs. A deep, ongoing cough is the main symptom. Bronchitis and many flu symptoms often are worse in people who smoke. Both pneumonia and bronchitis are serious illnesses that need a doctor's treatment.

Colds are more common in children than adults. Children get from 6 to 10 colds a year. If children are in school, the number of colds per child can go up to 12 per year. Adults average two to four colds each year.

Cold, Flu, or Something Else?

Many other disorders can act like a cold or flu. Here are some examples:

Allergy. Some people have allergic reactions to pollen, pet dander, dust, and other substances that can be breathed in. This can cause sniffles, sneezing, and sore throat. Sometimes a cold that lasts a long time is actually a mild allergy.

Acid reflux. With this condition, stomach acid backs up into the esophagus and throat. This problem affects many adults and some teens. If the acid constantly backs up, it can cause a feeling of burning in the throat. Sometimes the acid backup leads to bronchitis. Burning in the chest that worsens after eating, at night, or while lying down may mean acid reflux. People should see a doctor for chronic, or long-lasting, reflux.

Strep throat. Colds sometimes result in a mild sore throat. A severe sore throat combined with problems swallowing could be strep throat or another bacterial infection. This illness requires seeing a doctor for medicine.

Lyme disease. During the warmer months, some people have flu-like symptoms. This could be Lyme disease. This disease is transmitted by a bite from infected deer ticks. People who think they have Lyme disease should see a doctor for care.

Lyme disease, which is spread by the bite of an infected deer tick, imitates the flu.

The Mighty Flu Virus

In 412 B.C., Hippocrates described what was probably an epidemic of flu. An epidemic is the quick spread of a contagious disease within a certain population. The first recorded flu epidemic hit in 1580. Robert Johnson, a doctor in Philadelphia, was the first to provide detailed medical information about a flu epidemic in 1793. After that, doctors reported many flu epidemics.

The worst flu pandemic in recorded history struck near the end of World War I (1914–1918). A pandemic is an epidemic that covers a wide geographic area. In March 1918, a cook at Fort Riley, Kansas, reported chills and fever. Several days later, more than 500 other men at the military camp developed the same flu. Some became very ill. They had trouble breathing, sweated a lot, and their skin broke out with purple blisters. Some coughed constantly, others spit out cups of phlegm, or mucus. In all, 46 died from this flu at Camp Riley.

Some men infected with this flu went to France to help defend Europe during the war. The flu next spread from France to England and Spain. Then it moved even farther, to Germany, Russia, India, China, Japan, Africa, South America, and Alaska. Finally, the pandemic disappeared in early 1919. Even today, no one knows how or why this pandemic started.

In the 10 months this flu lasted, it caused great suffering. Worldwide, about 2 billion people had been sick. Of those, 20 million died. In the United States, 25 million caught the virus and 500,000 died. In Canada, 30,000 to 50,000 people died. No war in history has caused this many deaths.

Worldwide flu pandemics have continued to strike. During 1957 and 1958, the Asian flu caused 70,000 deaths in the United States. Nearly 10 years later, from 1968–1969, the Hong Kong flu caused 34,000 deaths in the United States. Other pandemics have struck since then.

Ever-Changing Flu Virus

Two facts make it tricky to develop drugs to stop flu viruses from spreading. First, over time, flu viruses change by mutation. That means they change their genetic material. These small changes allow the flu virus to enter the body and get past the immune system. The antibodies for old flu viruses don't work against this newly changed virus. So, people can get the flu again and again.

Second, old and new flu viruses spread easily from person to person. They also can spread from animal or bird to person, or vice versa.

Myth: The flu virus dies once it's outside the body.

Fact: The flu virus can stay in the air for as long as three hours. Some viruses can be dormant, or inactive, for days, months, or even years.

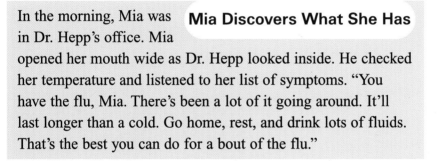

Mia Discovers What She Has

In the morning, Mia was in Dr. Hepp's office. Mia opened her mouth wide as Dr. Hepp looked inside. He checked her temperature and listened to her list of symptoms. "You have the flu, Mia. There's been a lot of it going around. It'll last longer than a cold. Go home, rest, and drink lots of fluids. That's the best you can do for a bout of the flu."

Points to Consider

Why do you think fall is the start of the flu season?

Why do you think children get more colds than adults do?

How do you think the flu spreads so quickly from person to person?

How do you think a pandemic spreads from country to country?

What would you be able to tell someone who seems to be getting a cold or the flu?

Chapter Overview

Viruses cause many diseases. Many of these diseases still affect people in North America and worldwide. Others have been controlled.

The nervous system can suffer from various viral infections. Sometimes these can become serious if not treated early.

Viruses that infect the glands cause mumps and mononucleosis. These diseases seldom cause serious problems.

Smallpox, measles, chicken pox, and German measles are viral diseases of the skin.

Hepatitis is a serious infection of the liver. Hepatitis B (HBV) affects many teens and young adults. It can result in liver cancer or death from liver failure.

Two sexually transmitted diseases are genital herpes and AIDS. Both are caused by viruses. These diseases can be treated but not cured.

Chapter 4

Other Viral Diseases

Viruses cause many diseases that can affect different parts of the body. Many of these diseases affect people worldwide every year. Others such as smallpox and polio have been controlled.

Viral Diseases of the Nervous System

The nervous system can suffer from a variety of viral infections. Some can become serious if not discovered and treated early.

Encephalitis

Encephalitis is an inflammation of the brain. A virus carried by an infected mosquito sometimes causes encephalitis. This disease typically starts with a headache and fever. If not treated, a person can become confused and see and hear imaginary things. The person may even become paralyzed, or unable to move. Speech, memory, behavior, and vision problems can occur. A small number of people can go into a coma, or state of unconsciousness, and die. However, most people recover completely.

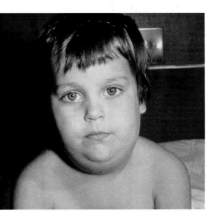

Mumps causes the salivary glands that are near the ears to swell.

Viral Meningitis

Viral meningitis is inflammation of the membranes that cover the brain and spinal cord. Viral meningitis usually produces mild flu-like symptoms. This viral disease requires no treatment. However, symptoms sometimes are severe. Then, the person may have to see a doctor to make sure the illness isn't bacterial meningitis. Bacterial meningitis is fast acting and can cause death.

Poliomyelitis

Poliomyelitis, or polio, once caused much fear. This viral disease can lead to paralysis, shrunken limbs, and sometimes death. It can paralyze the breathing muscles, making machines necessary to keep the person breathing. Polio strikes young children the hardest.

Polio epidemics rolled across the United States and worldwide for many years. Polio epidemics increased by the 1950s. In the United States, 1952 ranked as the worst year for polio. About 58,000 people became infected, 21,000 were paralyzed, and more than 3,000 died.

During the 1950s, medical researchers Jonas Salk and Albert Sabin, working separately, developed a polio vaccine. Their vaccine caused the body to produce antibodies to the virus. Polio became a disease of history in North America and Europe during the 1990s. Worldwide vaccination against polio continues, but some polio cases occur in the Caribbean and Asia.

Viral Diseases of the Glands

Viruses that infect the glands cause mumps and mononucleosis. These diseases bring discomfort but seldom cause serious problems.

Mumps

A virus that attacks the glands causes mumps. The salivary glands near the ears swell and the person develops round, puffy checks. The disease affects people worldwide and is highly contagious. It strikes children between the ages of 5 and 9 most often but can attack all ages. Fewer than 5,000 people in the United States get mumps each year. A vaccine for mumps is available in the combined measles-mumps-rubella (MMR) vaccine.

Mononucleosis

Mononucleosis is a viral infection that can be common among teens. Symptoms include chills, fever, sore throat, tiredness, and swollen lymph nodes. Lymph nodes contain lymph, a colorless liquid that carries white blood cells. Often called mono or the kissing disease, mononucleosis spreads through direct contact such as kissing. Complete bed rest is needed to recover. The disease can last from three to six weeks. Some teens need three to six months before they can return to competitive sport activities.

Caryn, Age 15

"I need to sit down," Caryn said. She and Thu were shopping at the mall.

"You don't look good," said Thu. "Are you getting the flu?"

"I don't know what I have, but I woke up with a sore throat. I feel cold, like I can't warm up. I'm sorry, Thu, but I need to go home and crawl into bed. I'm so tired."

Thu nodded. "Isn't your boyfriend, Ari, sick, too? Maybe you have the kissing disease!"

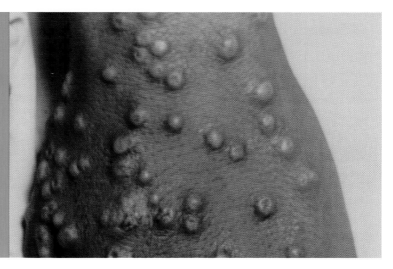

Viral Diseases of the Skin

Several types of viral diseases affect the skin. These include smallpox, measles, chicken pox, and German measles.

Smallpox

Smallpox is a very contagious disease that often causes death. When first sick, people run a high fever. Then they develop a rash on the face, the palms, and the soles of the feet. Over the next 6 to 10 days, the rash develops into red, painful pimples. Bacteria sometimes infect the pimples. As people recover, the pimples crust and often leave scars. Some people die from infection of the lungs, heart, or brain.

Smallpox epidemics occurred in ancient Greece, China, Korea, and Japan. The disease spread throughout the world, and until the 1960s, smallpox continued to kill millions. In 1967, the United Nations World Health Organization (WHO) began a worldwide vaccination campaign against smallpox. By mid-1975, only a few cases were left in two countries, Bangladesh and Ethiopia. The WHO recorded the disappearance of smallpox from the Earth in 1980.

Very contagious viral diseases such as measles and chicken pox are spread through the air. They're spread by infected water droplets released by talking, coughing, and sneezing.

Fast
Fact

Measles

Like smallpox, measles is very contagious. It can occur at any age but mainly affects children. Measles starts with a fever, runny nose, irritated eyes, and coughing. A red rash appears three or four days later and covers the entire body. In a few days, the rash starts to clear and the fever goes down. Sometimes the skin peels. Measles can result in ear and chest infections. More serious complications can develop, such as encephalitis or even death.

Measles was once a common childhood disease in North America. It became much less frequent after a vaccine was developed in 1963. In other parts of the world, measles is still a common disease among children.

Chicken Pox

Chicken pox rates as another very contagious disease. Like measles, it mainly strikes children. The disease starts with a fever, followed by the appearance of itchy red spots all over the body. Chicken pox is rarely dangerous for most children. However, it can cause serious problems in children with certain diseases such as cancer. Adults who get chicken pox sometimes become very ill. Most doctors recommend that children who have not had the disease be vaccinated against it.

The virus that causes chicken pox can remain alive but hidden in the nerves. Decades later, the virus may multiply within the body and cause another disease called shingles. This painful skin rash has no cure.

German Measles

German measles also is called rubella. Symptoms include a rose-colored rash, slight fever, and sore throat. The lymph glands behind the ears swell. The rash, which lasts from one to three days, first appears on the face and spreads to the chest, limbs, and stomach. German measles was most common among teens and young adults. This disease is rarely seen today in the United States and Canada. The MMR vaccine protects against rubella.

Getting rubella can be a problem for women who are less than three months pregnant. When their baby is born, he or she may have heart defects, mental retardation, deafness, or vision problems. A rubella attack after the fifth month of pregnancy rarely causes birth defects.

Viral Disease of the Liver: Hepatitis

Hepatitis is inflammation of the liver. The severity of the infection depends on the type of virus, A, B, or C. Doctors have discovered new types of the virus as well. These are types D and E. Vaccines exist for types A and B.

Hepatitis B (HBV) is a serious liver disease that can lead to liver cancer or death. There is no cure. Hundreds of American teens are infected with this virus every week. The virus can be spread many ways. This includes having sex with an infected partner, sharing infected needles, or sharing personal items such as razors.

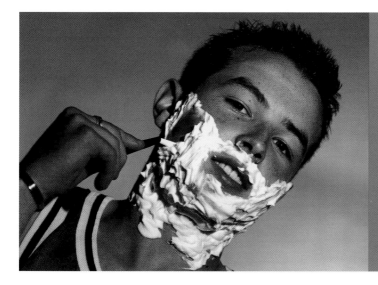

Sharing personal items such as razors can spread the hepatitis B virus.

Early symptoms of viral hepatitis are much like the flu. They include:

Fatigue, or tiredness

No appetite

Nausea (upset stomach)

Vomiting (throwing up)

Mild fever

Sore muscles and joints

Stomach pain

Later symptoms can include dark urine, or liquid body waste, and yellowish skin and eyes. Recovery from hepatitis is often slow, sometimes requiring three to six months.

"It's important to take care of yourself. That's why I use a condom every time I have sex. By doing this, I also show that I care for my partner."—Juan, age 18

Sexually Transmitted Viral Disease: Genital Herpes

Many young children get fever blisters or cold sores around the mouth. These are caused by infection with a virus called herpes simplex type 1. Fever blisters often reappear once or twice a year, but they don't cause serious illness in children. A closely related virus to herpes simplex type 1 is called herpes simplex type 2, or genital herpes.

In genital herpes, blisters or sores form on the penis, vagina, or anus. Sometimes the sores appear on a person's mouth. The blisters go away, but the person is still infected. The sores usually are painful and last one to three weeks. Some people never notice their sores. Some people have only one outbreak of blisters. Most people have blisters that return throughout their life.

Genital herpes is contagious and is spread through sexual contact with the infected area. It can be passed at any time, even if no sores are visible. A mother with an outbreak of genital herpes can pass it to her baby during childbirth. If this happens, the baby can have nervous system damage, blindness, or mental retardation. It may even result in death.

The drug acyclovir now is widely used in teens and adults who have genital herpes. Acyclovir doesn't cure genital herpes, but it can help prevent the disease's genital sores. The drug also is used to treat newborns who are infected at birth because their mother has genital herpes.

An unborn baby can get HIV from its mother. A newborn can become infected during childbirth.

Viral Disease of the Immune System: AIDS

The human immunodeficiency virus (HIV) was discovered in the 1980s. The virus lives in the cells of the immune system and eventually destroys it. When the immune system is weakened seriously, acquired immunodeficiency syndrome (AIDS) develops. A simple cold can become life threatening to someone with AIDS.

HIV is spread through the exchange of body fluids such as blood, vaginal discharge, and semen. Discharge is fluid that's released. Semen is fluid that contains sperm, the male sex cells. HIV can be passed from infected needles used for drugs, body piercing, or tattooing. Some drugs now are available to treat AIDS. However, AIDS has no cure.

Points to Consider

Why do you think mononucleosis also is called the kissing disease?

Why do you think the WHO recommended that laboratory stocks of the smallpox virus be destroyed?

Which viral diseases have you been vaccinated against?

What do you think is the best way to avoid getting herpes and AIDS?

Chapter Overview

Over-the-counter (OTC) medicines can help relieve the symptoms of flu or colds.

People shouldn't take antibiotics for flu or colds. Antibiotics only work on bacterial infections. Children and teens should never take aspirin if they have flu or chicken pox symptoms. Doing so could result in a serious disease called Reye's syndrome.

Some people try alternative remedies when they have a cold or flu. No evidence proves these help. People who want to use an alternative remedy should ask their doctor first.

Besides OTC medicines, other flu and cold treatments include getting rest and sleep and drinking plenty of liquids.

The best way to stop the spread of viruses is to wash your hands regularly.

The flu vaccine can protect people against some flu viruses.

Chapter 5

Treating and Preventing Flu and Colds

Armond blew his nose. Then he looked at the rows of colorful boxes on the drugstore's shelves. What was the best one to buy? He walked to the pharmacy counter and said to the pharmacist, "I want some relief for my cold. But what do I buy? This store carries so many cold remedies."

Armond, Age 16

The pharmacist laughed. "Yes, we carry shelves of them, but that's what I'm here for. I can help you pick out the right liquids, pills, capsules, tablets, or lozenges."

When a cold or flu strikes, many people are like Armond. They want relief but aren't sure what the best choices are. Many people also are not sure how to prevent flu and colds. There are a number of things they can do to help keep from getting these viruses.

Over-the-Counter Medicines

No proven cure exists for flu or colds. Over-the-counter (OTC) medicines are available to help relieve the symptoms. These products are available without a doctor's prescription, or written order. OTC medicines can make people feel more comfortable while they have the flu or a cold. These products treat the symptoms of minor conditions but do not treat the actual illness.

The following OTC products can help relieve certain symptoms of flu or colds. Many OTC cold and flu medicines contain a mix of the following four ingredients to attack multiple symptoms.

Nasal decongestants open up the passages in the nose. They're available as sprays or drops or can be taken by mouth. Using sprays or drops longer than three days can cause nasal stuffiness to worsen.

Antitussives or cough suppressants can quiet coughs. They're available as liquids or throat lozenges. They're also available as ointment that's rubbed on the chest or used in a vaporizer. A vaporizer changes liquid to mist.

Expectorants are taken by mouth. They help loosen mucus.

Antihistamines block the action of histamine on nasal passages. The body produces histamines during the flu or a cold. These chemicals cause sneezing, runny nose, and watery eyes. Antihistamines help the nose and eyes become less stuffy. They also help people to breathe more easily.

Some remedies contain other drugs, such as:

Caffeine, a stimulant to counter feeling tired. (It also helps other drugs in the same medicine work faster.)

Aspirin or acetaminophen (nonaspirin) to lower fever and relieve aching. (See section on Medicine Cautions that follows.)

Antacids to counter the stomach upset that aspirin can cause

Follow the product label and take no more than the prescribed amount of any OTC medicine. Do not take an OTC medicine for extended periods of time. If symptoms continue or do not get better, see a doctor.

OTC cold and flu medicines will not help someone get better faster. In fact, they can cause stomach upset or make the person dizzy, tired, or unable to sleep. Some doctors recommend not using OTC medicine to treat a cold or flu.

Medicine Cautions

Antibiotics shouldn't be taken to treat flu or colds. Antibiotics do not kill viruses. They should be used only for bacterial complications such as ear infections. Overuse of antibiotics has become a serious problem. This has led to bacteria becoming resistant to antibiotics, so these drugs are useless against bacteria.

Aspirin is one of the most common drugs available. It's listed under other names, too, including *choline salicylate, magnesium salicylate,* and *salicylic acid.*

Children and teens with symptoms of flu or chicken pox should not take aspirin or products containing aspirin. Using aspirin during a viral infection greatly increases the risk of Reye's syndrome. This serious illness usually affects children and teens. Adults also may be affected.

Reye's syndrome affects all organs of the body, especially the brain and liver. It causes pressure in the brain. The increased pressure causes brain cells to swell, and the brain can die from lack of blood. The illness also causes huge amounts of fat to develop in the liver and other organs.

Alternative Remedies

Some people say vitamin C or zinc prevents colds or relieves symptoms. There's no evidence to prove this. In fact, taking large amounts of any vitamin or mineral, such as zinc, may be harmful.

Various herbs are sometimes said to be cures for cold or flu. These include echinacea, ephedra, eucalyptus, garlic, ginger, and peppermint. These claims, however, have not been scientifically proven. If you want to try an herbal remedy, talk with your doctor first. Herbs can have side effects and can interact with other medicines.

Ephedra is an herb that has been used in China for more than 4,000 years. However, in the United States, the Food and Drug Administration (FDA) has received hundreds of reports of bad reactions to ephedra. These reactions have ranged from high blood pressure, sleep problems, and headaches, to seizures, heart attacks, strokes, and even death. As a result, some states have stopped all sales of herbal remedies containing ephedra.

Taking Care

If you do get a cold or flu, doctors advise plenty of bed rest. Your body is trying to attack the virus, and that takes energy. Resting gives your body a better chance to fight off the infection. Doctors also advise drinking at least 10 glasses of clear fluids a day for a flu or cold. This replaces fluids that you lose when the nose runs or the body sweats. Clear liquids include water, tea without caffeine, and chicken broth.

A warm bath or heating pad can soothe aches and pains. Steam from a hot shower can help you breathe more easily. Sleeping with your head elevated can help relieve congestion in the nose. Gargling with warm salt water can relieve a sore throat. Make the salt water by stirring ¼ teaspoon (1 gram) of salt into 8 ounces (240 milliliters) of warm water.

Cough and sneeze into a disposable tissue, then toss it. Get a new toothbrush after you've been sick. Also, wash towels and face cloths in hot water.

Stopping the Spread of Viruses

You can do many simple things to help stop the spread of flu and cold viruses.

Wash your hands regularly. This is the best way to stop the spread of cold and flu viruses. Wash before and after meals and after using the bathroom. To wash, use soap, work up bubbles, then rinse with warm water.

Get regular exercise and enough rest. This can help keep your body fit and strong, so you can better fight off illnesses.

Try not to rub your eyes and nose. For example, you may wipe your nose with your hand or sneeze or cough into your hand. If you have a cold or flu, you move the virus onto your skin by doing this. If other people touch your hand, they can get the cold or flu virus onto their hands, face, nose, or eyes.

If you're sick, do not share your food, drinks, toothbrush, washcloth, towels, cups, or eating utensils. You can easily pass on your virus this way. Use disposable tissues, not handkerchiefs. Cold and flu viruses can live for some time on cloth handkerchiefs. Throw used tissues into the trash right away.

You can spread your cold or flu from the moment you get sick until the virus leaves your body. People who have a cold or flu are most contagious when symptoms are getting worse. That's usually within a couple days of the start of the cold or flu.

Stay away or stand back from others if you have a cold or flu. If you have a cold or flu, cover your mouth when you cough. Turn away when you blow your nose into a tissue.

Any kind of soap is fine for washing hands. Antibacterial soaps kill only bacteria, not viruses. However, washing can remove viruses from your hands.

Flu Vaccines

Some people get a flu vaccine in the fall to protect against getting the flu. Given as a shot, a vaccine puts a small amount of killed flu virus into the body. The amount is so tiny that people do not get sick. Instead the body prepares itself against getting the flu.

However, this vaccine doesn't protect against all flu viruses and must be given each year. Some people still get the flu even if they get the vaccine. Health experts say the flu shot is 70 to 90 percent effective in preventing the flu. Your doctor can advise if you need a flu shot.

Points to Consider

How could you encourage a young child with a cold or flu to stay in bed and rest?

What could you do to lift the spirits of a friend who is having a bad bout of flu?

Why do you think people try scientifically unproven ways to treat a cold or flu?

Do your family members get an annual flu shot? After reading this chapter, what information could you give them?

Chapter Overview

Many myths exist about colds and flu.

Flu vaccines generally are recommended for most people.

Vaccines usually are very safe medicines.

Chapter 6

Viruses and Vaccines:
True or False?

Test your knowledge about colds, flu, viruses, and vaccines with these three sets of true or false questions.

Colds and Flu: True or False?

Damp, cold, or drafty weather causes colds. **False.** Colds depend on people's contact with each other to spread the virus, not on the weather.

Working up a sweat can flush out a cold. **False.** During exercise, getting sweaty may make people with a cold feel better for a while. Breathing warm, moist air can help, too. In both instances, congestion in the head and nose loosens. However, the only way to get rid of a cold is to wait until the body fights it off.

It's best to stop coughs. False. Unless coughing interferes with sleep, it is best *to* cough. Coughing helps get rid of mucus that builds up in the lungs and clogs airways.

Cleaning and disinfecting kitchen and bathroom counters helps protect against spreading cold and flu viruses. (Disinfectants are chemicals used to kill germs.) **True.** Cold and flu viruses can live for hours on hands. They also can live for a time on hard surfaces such as countertops, wood, and plastic. Washing hands or surfaces with soap and water generally removes most viruses. However, some experts believe use of disinfectants such as antibacterial products is helping new kinds of germs to develop. These germs may cause diseases that are hard to fight with existing medicines.

Chicken soup can help relieve cold symptoms. **True.** Having some hot chicken soup can help clear mucous particles from the nose. Removing these particles that contain viruses is part of the body's defense against germs. Also, chicken soup can soothe a sore throat, unstuff a clogged nose, and replace lost body fluids. At the end of this section you will find a recipe for homemade chicken soup.

Colds usually come on slowly. **True.** Symptoms develop one to three days after exposure to the virus. These include a runny or stuffy nose, sneezing, and sore throat.

Influenza and Other Viruses

Flu-related costs total about $12 billion a year for health care in the United States.

Fast Fact

People catch a cold more easily if they have wet hair in cold weather. **False.**

No medicines are available to prevent the flu. **False.** In general, antiviral drugs can lessen the impact of viruses. For example, two antiviral drugs can help reduce the length and severity of type A flu. They are called amantadine and rimantadine. Both are taken by mouth. Only people who are at high risk for type A flu should take these powerful and costly medicines.

You can spread a cold or flu virus from the moment you feel sick until the virus leaves your body. **True.** People with a cold or flu are most contagious when their symptoms begin. This often is when they are sneezing and have a runny nose.

The old saying, "Feed a cold, starve a fever," is true. **False.** Eating healthy foods and drinking plenty of clear liquids helps fight off a cold or flu. People with a cold or flu or fever may not be too hungry, but they need to eat a little.

At the first sign of a cold or flu, see a doctor. **False.** For most people, there's no need to see a doctor. The body can fight off most colds and flu. However, if symptoms don't go away or get worse after three or four days, do see a doctor. Also, see your doctor if breathing is painful or difficult or if you have a high fever.

Myth: Everyone gets a cold at least once a year.

Fact: Some people never get colds. In fact, about 10 percent of adults do not get colds. Scientists do not know why these people are so lucky!

Easy Chicken Noodle Soup

1 20-ounce (570-gram) package chicken breast with bones and skin
1 medium carrot, peeled and chopped into bite-sized pieces
1 medium onion, peeled and chopped into bite-sized pieces
1 celery stalk, chopped into bite-sized pieces (optional)
4 cups (.95 liters) water
1 teaspoon (5 grams) salt, or to taste
⅛ teaspoon (625 milligrams) black pepper, or to taste
1 cup (225 grams) medium egg noodles, cooked until just tender (follow the package directions), and drained
2 tablespoons (30 grams) parsley, chopped (optional)

Put chicken, carrot, onion, celery, water, salt, and pepper into a large saucepan and bring to a boil over high heat. Cover and reduce the heat to low. Simmer for 90 minutes. Remove the chicken, using tongs or another kitchen utensil. Toss the bones and skin and shred the chicken into bite-sized pieces. Put the chicken pieces into the soup.

Divide the noodles among four soup bowls. Ladle the chicken soup over the noodles. Top with parsley if desired. Serves 4.

Flu Vaccines: True or False?

The best time to get the flu vaccine is mid-October to mid-November. **True.** This is just before the flu season hits. It takes the immune system about six to eight weeks to respond to the vaccine.

Flu vaccines usually are inexpensive and available at most doctors' offices, health agencies, and pharmacies. Some companies now offer vaccines to their workers. Some organizations offer the vaccine at convenient places such as malls or grocery stores.

"The grocery store is offering flu shots now. Should I take Damon and we'll both get one?" Kwame asked his dad.

Kwame, Age 16

"That's nice of you to offer, Kwame. Since you got your driver's license, you've been great about running errands," said his dad. "But . . ."

Kwame interrupted, "But you're going to tell me no."

"You can't get the vaccine because you're allergic to eggs. Your little brother can get one and so can I. Here are the keys. You're driving!"

Everyone should get a flu vaccine. **False.** Not everyone can get a flu vaccine safely. Children younger than 6 months should not get this shot. People allergic to eggs cannot get the vaccine. That's because the vaccine is made from viruses grown in chicken eggs. People with certain allergies and medical problems should talk with their doctor before getting the shot. Those with a high fever need to wait until they feel better and the fever lowers before getting vaccinated.

The flu vaccine can cause side effects. **True.** Side effects are rare. The most common side effect is soreness at the shot site for one to two days. Some people may develop a mild fever, sore muscles, headache, and tiredness that last one or two days.

Fast Fact

By first grade, children in the United States usually have received as many as **10** different vaccines. This totals **19** shots.

The flu vaccine cannot cause flu. **True.** That's because it doesn't contain live flu viruses.

If I got a flu vaccine last year, I don't need one this year. **False.** There are two reasons why people need an annual flu shot. (1) Flu viruses constantly change, so vaccines must be taken each year. (2) Flu antibody levels decrease over time, so antibody levels are low one year after a vaccine.

About 90 percent of North Americans get a flu shot. **False.** Less than half of the people who could benefit the most from this vaccine get one. This includes people older than 50 and those with chronic health problems, such as severe asthma.

Vaccines: True or False?

All vaccines are made from killed or dead viruses. **False.** Some examples of vaccines that contain killed viruses are flu, hepatitis B, and rabies vaccines. Other vaccines are made from live, weakened viruses. These include chicken pox and measles-mumps-rubella (MMR) vaccines.

Only children need immunizations, or vaccine shots. **False.** Adults also need to be vaccinated from time to time to protect themselves against serious diseases. Adults need shots for flu, tetanus, diphtheria, and chicken pox, as well as measles-mumps-rubella. Tetanus happens when a wound becomes infected with bacteria. Diphtheria causes inflammation of the heart and nervous system.

Vaccines are among the safest medicines available. **True.** Sometimes mild side effects occur such as a sore arm or low fever. As with any medicine, serious problems can develop, but the risk is very low.

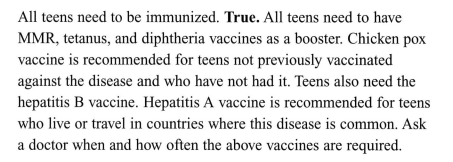
As with drugs, vaccines must undergo much testing to prove they're safe and effective. In the United States, the Food and Drug Administration must first approve a new vaccine. Then the Centers for Disease Control and Prevention (CDC), the American Academy of Pediatrics (AAP), and the American Academy of Family Physicians (AAFP) must recommend it.

All teens need to be immunized. **True.** All teens need to have MMR, tetanus, and diphtheria vaccines as a booster. Chicken pox vaccine is recommended for teens not previously vaccinated against the disease and who have not had it. Teens also need the hepatitis B vaccine. Hepatitis A vaccine is recommended for teens who live or travel in countries where this disease is common. Ask a doctor when and how often the above vaccines are required.

Teens need to keep a personal immunization record. **True.** Staying up-to-date on immunizations can help protect teens against certain diseases.

Points to Consider

Before you read this chapter, what myths did you believe about flu and colds?

How can you find out where and when the flu vaccine will be given in your area?

How would you help promote the awareness of proper immunizations for children and teens?

Why do you think it's important to keep a list of your medical exams and vaccines?

Chapter Overview

Prevention of viral diseases now is more effective than at any time in the past. Smallpox has been wiped out on the Earth. Scientists are targeting polio and measles next.

Researchers can act quickly to prevent global spreading of new viral diseases, thanks to viral monitoring.

Researchers are working on new types of flu-fighting drugs. These drugs shorten the length of flu symptoms and also may prevent the flu.

Much current vaccine research is focused on new types of vaccines that do not inject entire live or killed viruses. Instead they use other methods that cause fewer side effects.

A top priority in virus research is HIV and AIDS.

Chapter 7

Looking Ahead

Doctors and researchers now know more about disease-causing viruses than ever before. Prevention now is more effective than at any time in the past. Scientists also are continuing research into viruses and are working on new vaccines and other ways to fight viruses.

Disappearance of Viral Diseases

Smallpox was the first viral disease to be conquered. Worldwide vaccines wiped out this once-dreaded disease. The World Health Organization has targeted the polio and measles viruses next. Many people and organizations are carrying on this amazing work of vaccinating people worldwide. This includes the WHO and other health organizations, as well as medical doctors, nurses, and drug companies.

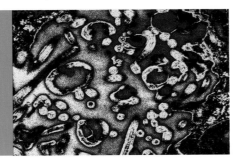

The Ebola virus is a deadly new virus being watched for by workers at monitoring stations.

The WHO plans to eliminate polio worldwide by 2005. To do this, almost all people of the world will need to be vaccinated. In 1994, about 80 percent of children worldwide younger than age 1 received a polio vaccine. By the next year, half of the world's children younger than age 5 were immunized. These vaccines are working. In 1996, only 2,090 people worldwide developed polio.

Measles is the third viral disease targeted by the WHO. Measles kills more children than all other diseases preventable by vaccines. However, this virus is hard to eliminate for two reasons. First, the measles vaccine does not work for infants, or babies. Second, many people throughout the world are not vaccinated against measles. Some African and Asian countries, France, and Italy still have large numbers of people who aren't vaccinated.

Viral Watchdogs

People at monitoring stations worldwide watch for new viruses. They also look for the return of well-known types. The recent appearance of bleeding fever viruses such as Ebola as well as HIV has provided researchers with major challenges.

Recently, the United States Centers for Disease Control and Prevention has focused on Hong Kong. A new flu strain may be developing there. Researchers from the United States and Hong Kong are working together to track down the new flu virus. Called "bird flu," this virus spreads from chickens to people or from people to people and can cause death. Researchers worry that this new viral flu could travel quickly throughout the world.

Influenza and Other Viruses

Flu vaccines are made from proteins on the surface of the virus. Because these proteins change yearly, the vaccine also must be changed, and people need a new vaccine each year. Belgian scientists have developed a vaccine made from a protein present every year in most strains of type A flu. This vaccine provides long-lasting protection in mice. If this works for people, then annual flu shots may not be needed. Such a vaccine for humans is years away from becoming available.

Justin, Age 16

Justin has a new career goal. He just read an article about the Centers for Disease Control (CDC) virus fighters. These people can be asked to go anywhere at any time. They often put in 14 to 18 hours a day of work. Their mission is to examine and prevent outbreaks of new, unusual, or common dangerous diseases. Justin likes the idea of helping to save the world from a major disease outbreak. He said, "It'd be exciting to be the first to know about something that could threaten the world's health. And what's better, I could do something to help."

New Flu-Fighting Drugs

Researchers are developing a new type of flu-fighting drug. These drugs, called neuraminidase inhibitors, shorten the length of a bout of the flu. They work on both type A and B flu by preventing the virus from forming its outer coat.

In 1999, zanamivir (Relenza) became the first of these drugs to be released in the United States. It can be used for people ages 12 and older who have the flu. The drug is inhaled through a device similar to an asthma inhaler. It works best in people who have been vaccinated and must be taken on the first day of flu symptoms. Then, it's taken for five days. The drug is costly and is used mostly by elderly people.

That same year, oseltamivir (Tamiflu) became the second new drug available to shorten how long flu symptoms last. This drug also may help people avoid getting the flu. Other flu-fighting drugs are scheduled for release in 2002 and beyond.

New Vaccine Research

Much current vaccine research is focused on new types of vaccines. These new vaccines do not involve injecting entire live or killed viruses into the body. Instead, they use other methods. One method is to inject only the outer shell of the virus. This seems to be enough for the body to create antibodies. Another method involves part of a virus created in a laboratory. This artificial virus fools the body into thinking that a real virus is invading. The body then produces antibodies.

Researchers are working on a third approach. This vaccine uses only a tiny part of a virus called a subunit virus. The first subunit vaccine in the United States is for hepatitis B. This vaccine works well, and doctors throughout the world now use it for newborns. Currently, researchers are working on subunit vaccines for measles.

The main benefit of all these new methods is the lowered risk of side effects from vaccination. The risk of infection also is greatly reduced.

Research for new vaccines may help lower the risk of side effects and infection from vaccinations.

HIV and AIDS Research

One of the top priorities for virus research is HIV and AIDS. HIV is probably the most studied virus in history. After years of research and testing of various medicines, researchers are still trying to prevent and treat HIV and AIDS.

Much AIDS research has focused on T-cell lymphocytes. T-cells attack germs and also help control the activity of the immune system. Scientists are researching drugs or other treatments that increase the activity of T-cells. They also hope to find drugs that stop the spread of the HIV virus from one T-cell to another.

Points to Consider

How could you help people who are affected by a serious viral disease?

Why do you think it can take years for new drugs to be approved for human use?

Do you think the WHO will be able to wipe out polio and measles? Why or why not?

Why do you think HIV is the most studied virus in history?

Glossary

antibody (AN-ti-bod-ee)—protein produced by the body to help fight disease and infection; lymphocytes in the immune system produce antibodies.

bacteria (bak-TIHR-ee-uh)—microscopic living things that exist all around; some bacteria are useful, others can cause disease.

communicable (kuh-MYOO-nuh-kuh-buhl)—easily spread from person to person

contagious (kuhn-TAY-juhss)—capable of being spread by coming into contact with a person or thing that is infected

electron microscope (i-LEK-tron MYE-kruh-skope)—a microscope that uses electron rays to produce a very high magnification

epidemic (ep-uh-DEM-ik)—the quick spread of a communicable disease throughout a population

immune system (i-MYOON SISS-tuhm)—the system that protects the body from illness and disease

inflammation (in-fluh-MAY-shuhn)—redness, heat, swelling, and pain

lymphocyte (LIM-fuh-site)—a white blood cell that either multiplies and attacks germs or makes antibodies

mucus (MYOO-kuhss)—the clear, slippery liquid of mucous membranes; mucus moistens, cleans, and protects.

mutation (myoo-TAY-shuhn)—a change in the genes of viruses or living things

symptom (SIMP-tuhm)—evidence of an illness or medical condition

vaccine (vak-SEEN)—a liquid containing a weakened or killed virus; a vaccine helps the immune system fight off a disease before a person gets it.

virus (VYE-ruhss)—a tiny germ that grows in living cells and can cause disease

For More Information

Altman, Linda. *Plague and Pestilence: A History of Infectious Disease.* Springfield, NJ: Enslow, 1998.

Aronson, Virginia. *The Influenza Pandemic of 1918.* Philadelphia: Chelsea House, 2000.

Dudley, William, and Mary E. Williams, eds. *Epidemics: Opposing Viewpoints.* San Diego, CA: Greenhaven Press, 1999.

Edelson, Edward. *The Immune System.* Philadelphia: Chelsea House, 2000.

Facklam, Howard, and Margery Facklam. *Viruses.* New York: 21st Century Books, 1994.

Hundley, David H. *Viruses.* Vero Beach, FL: Rourke Press, 1998.

 At publication, all resources listed here were accurate and appropriate to the topics covered in this book. Addresses and phone numbers may change. When visiting Internet sites and links, use good judgment. Remember, never give personal information over the Internet.

Useful Addresses and Internet Sites

American Social Health Association
PO Box 13827
Research Triangle Park, NC 27709-3827
www.ashastd.org

Centers for Disease Control and Prevention
1600 Clifton Road Northeast
Atlanta, GA 30333
www.cdc.gov

Health Canada
Division of STD Prevention & Control
Bureau of HIV/AIDS and STD
Brooke Claxton Building
Tunney's Pasture, Postal Locator 0900 B1
Ottawa, ON K1A 0K9
CANADA
www.hc-sc.gc.ca/hpb/lcdc/bah/std/index.html

National Foundation for Infectious Diseases
4733 Bethesda Avenue, Suite 750
Bethesda, MD 20814
www.nfid.org

The Big Picture Book of Viruses
www.tulane.edu/~dmsander/Big_Virology/BVHomePage.html
Offers a catalog of virus pictures

Health Canada: Flu Club
www.hc-sc.gc.ca/real/flu
Contains information about the flu

Health Finder
www.healthfinder.gov
Has information from the U.S. Department of Health and Human Services on viral diseases

Hidden Killers: Virus Basics
http://library.thinkquest.org/23054/basics/page5.html
Provides a history of viruses, as well as games and vocabulary

InteliHealth
www.intelihealth.com (Type "flu" in search space. Then, click on Flu-O-Meter.)
Offers a state-by-state map of where the flu currently is reported in the United States

KidsHealth
www.kidshealth.org/teen/health_problems/index.html
Contains articles on many different infections, including flu, encephalitis, mononucleosis, and HIV and AIDS

CDC National Immunization Information Hot Line
1-800-232-2522 (English)
1-800-232-0233 (Spanish)

National AIDS Hot Line
1-800-342-AIDS (800-342-2437)
1-800-344-7432 (Spanish)

STD Hot Line
1-800-227-8922

Index

Index continued